CW01202729

HEALTHY KIDS

EAT HEALTHY FOOD

by ANGELA ROYSTON
Illustrated by DAVIDE ORTU

W
FRANKLIN WATTS
LONDON·SYDNEY

First published in Great Britain in 2024 by Hodder & Stoughton

Copyright © Hodder & Stoughton Limited, 2024
(Text has previously appeared in *Being Healthy, Feeling Great: Diet* (2009), but has been updated for this edition.)

All rights reserved.

Credits
Series Editor: Amy Pimperton
Series Designer: Peter Scoulding
Consultants: Sue Beck MSc, BSc and Dr Kristina Routh

ISBN: 978 1 4451 8815 7 (hardback)
ISBN: 978 1 4451 8816 4 (paperback)

Printed in Dubai

MIX
Paper from responsible sources
FSC® C104740
www.fsc.org

Franklin Watts
An imprint of
Hachette Children's Group
Part of Hodder & Stoughton
Carmelite House
50 Victoria Embankment
London EC4Y 0DZ

An Hachette UK Company
www.hachette.co.uk
www.hachettechildrens.co.uk

The website addresses (URLs) included in this book were valid at the time of going to press. However, because of the nature of the Internet, it is possible that some addresses may have changed, or sites may have changed or closed down since publication. While the author and Publisher regret any inconvenience this may cause the readers, no responsibility for any such changes can be accepted by either the author or the Publisher.

CONTENTS

Why do you need to eat?	4
A balancing act	6
Food for energy	8
Beware of sugar!	10
Protein: the body's building blocks	12
Facts about fats	14
Vitamins and minerals	16
Regular fibre	18
Water	20
Eating too much	22
Eating too little	24
A healthy diet	26
Make a healthy pizza!	28
Quiz	29
Glossary	30
Find out more	31
Index	32

NOTE:

If you have any worries around eating, food and your mental health, please speak to a trusted adult, such as a parent, carer or teacher. They can help you to seek help from a doctor or other medical professional.

WHY DO YOU NEED TO EAT?

Food is essential for life. It gives you energy and it contains nutrients that you need to grow and be healthy. Your body breaks down and digests the nutrients in food, which your blood then carries to every part of your body.

NUTRIENTS

Nutrients are chemicals that your body needs. For example, foods such as sweet potatoes are rich in carbohydrates. Your body uses the carbohydrates for energy (see pages 6 and 8).

All the parts of your body, from your hair to your bones are made of different proteins (see pages 12–13). Your body uses proteins from food, such as fish, to make the proteins in your body.

FEELING HUNGRY?

You feel hungry when your stomach is empty and your body is low on energy. When you are hungry, the smell of food makes your mouth water with extra saliva. When you eat, your teeth chew each mouthful of food. The saliva mixes with the food to make a mushy ball, which you swallow.

DIGESTING

The food you swallow goes into your stomach. Here, special acids mix with it and turn it into a kind of thick 'soup', called chyme. This then slowly passes into your small intestine, where it is broken up into separate nutrients. The nutrients are so tiny that they pass through the walls of the small intestine into the blood. The rest passes on through the large intestine and becomes solid waste, called faeces.

FOOD FACT

Most food stays in your mouth for less than a minute, but it can stay in your stomach for up to four hours. It can then take another 20 hours to pass through your small and large intestines. This is because your intestines are very long – about three times as long as your height from head to toe.

A BALANCING ACT

The food you normally eat is called your diet. To eat healthily, you need to eat most of your food from four main food groups: carbohydrates; fruit and vegetables; protein and dairy food. You can also eat a small amount of food from a fifth food group: sugar and fat.

CARBOHYDRATES

Cereals and potatoes are starchy foods that contain carbohydrates. Cereals are grains, such as wheat, oats and rice. Breakfast cereals are made from grains. Wheat is used to make pasta and bread.

HEALTHY HINT

All the colours!

You should try to eat a colourful variety of fresh fruits and vegetables. The more colourful your diet, the more types of nutrient you are eating.

FRUIT AND VEGETABLES

Fruit and vegetables contain lots of vitamins, minerals and fibre (see pages 16–19). Fresh, raw fruit and vegetables contain the most nutrients, but cooked, frozen, dried and tinned vegetables are good, too.

DAIRY FOODS

Dairy is milk and food made from milk, such as cheese and yoghurt. Dairy food contains protein, as well as important vitamins and minerals, such as calcium (see page 16).

MEAT, FISH AND ALTERNATIVES

Meat and fish contain protein. People who are vegetarian do not eat meat or fish. Instead, they eat protein-rich foods such as eggs, nuts and beans. These are healthy foods for everyone.

SUGAR AND FAT

Some foods, such as fruit, contain natural sugar. Processed sugar is added to other foods, such as cakes, to make them taste sweet. If you'd like a little of something sweet, fruit is a much healthier choice than cake.

Many types of food contain fat. For example, beef may have streaks of fat running through it. You need to include a small amount of fat in your diet. Some fats, such as olive oil, are healthier than others. Choose these whenever you can.

FOOD FACT

For vegans, who eat only plants, soya is a great substitute for dairy protein. Tofu (soya bean curd) and soya milk are popular choices to replace cheese and milk.

FOOD FOR ENERGY

Starchy carbohydrates are foods that give you energy. Bread contains lots of starchy carbohydrates. If you chew a piece of bread, you will notice that it begins to taste sweet. That is because your saliva changes some of the starch in the bread into sugar. Your body breaks down the rest of the starch inside your body, turning it into a kind of sugar called glucose. This then goes into your blood and around your body to give you energy.

USING ENERGY

Every activity you do uses energy. You need energy to move about, to think – and even to sleep. Some of your energy is needed for physical exercise. People who are very active need to eat more starchy carbohydrates. Professional footballers and other athletes often eat starchy foods, such as pasta, a few hours before they take part in a match or competition.

ENERGY DIPS

You may begin to feel tired a few hours after eating. This is because once your body has digested all the starchy food, your blood is now running low on glucose. This tired feeling is often called an 'energy dip'.

TOP UP

A healthy snack to top up your energy will make you feel better. Dried fruits, such as dates, are a good snack. Fruit contains natural sugar, which your body digests quickly. This gives you an instant burst of energy. A banana is also a great snack, because it contains starch as well as sugar. This makes your energy last even longer.

HEALTHY HINT

Healthy snacks

Instead of crisps or chocolate, choose a healthy option, such as plain popcorn, an apple, carrot sticks, unsalted nuts, a hard-boiled egg or some natural yogurt with fresh fruit.

BEWARE OF SUGAR!

Processed sugar is used to sweeten fizzy drinks, cakes, chocolate and other sweet food. Without sugar, these foods and drinks would not taste as nice. Many people enjoy sugary foods because sugar tastes good and gives them energy. However, for many reasons, sugar is not a healthy choice.

SUGAR HIGHS?

Some people say that eating or drinking lots of sugary things can make them feel hyperactive. This is when you find it hard to sit still or concentrate, as the sugar levels in your blood go up.

... AND SUGAR LOWS

And because energy from sugar does not last long, the energy dip afterwards may leave you tired and bad-tempered. Researchers are still studying 'sugar crashes', but what we do know is that it is much better to eat fruit if you feel like something sweet. Fruit contains other nutrients and fibre, and keeps your energy levels up for longer.

TOOTH DECAY

Some of the sugar in sweet foods and drinks stays in your mouth after you have swallowed. The sugar clings to your teeth and gums. Bacteria in your mouth feed on the sugar and produce a kind of acid, which then attacks your teeth. The acid can make holes in your teeth. This is called tooth decay and it can be painful.

BANISH BAD BREATH

The bacteria in your mouth also produce a white, sticky substance, called plaque. Plaque makes your breath smell bad. It can also cause gum disease. You can protect your teeth and gums by cleaning them well. It is best to do this at least twice a day: morning and night.

HEALTHY HINT

Sugar solutions

You can also protect your teeth by eating less sugar. If you do eat or drink something sugary, try to clean your teeth shortly afterwards. If this is not possible, drink some water to help wash the sugar out of your mouth.

PROTEIN: the body's building blocks

Proteins are essential for good health. Hair, skin, muscles and other parts of the body are all made of different kinds of protein. It is good to eat a variety of protein-rich foods, so that your body is as healthy as possible.

PROTEIN FROM MEAT

If you eat meat, most will contain all the protein your body needs. Some meat, such as beef and lamb, contains a lot of fat, too, which can be unhealthy. It is good to eat different kinds of meat, rather than just one kind. Try to eat chicken and other poultry, such as turkey, too.

Fish is a good source of protein for your body because it does not contain much fat. Some fish, such as mackerel and sardines, are called oily fish. These are part of a healthy diet because they contain omega oils and other important nutrients.

NON-MEAT PROTEIN

Vegetarians and vegans can eat cheese (non-dairy cheese for vegans), nuts and pulses to get the proteins they need. Pulses include beans, chickpeas and lentils. Some vegetarians eat eggs, too.

Vegetarian protein is not as complete as meat or fish protein. This means that it does not contain all the different types of protein your body needs in just one type of food. By eating different kinds of vegetarian protein throughout your day or combined in one meal, you can make it more complete. For example, you can eat a nut burger with cheese on top.

HEALTHY HINT

Too salty!

Peanuts contain lots of protein. However, salted peanuts contain up to four times as much salt as meat or chicken. Too much salt is bad for your health (see page 17), so choose unsalted peanuts instead.

FACTS ABOUT FATS

Fat is found naturally in some foods, such as meat and avocados. Butter contains a lot of fat and so does oil, such as sunflower oil. People often use butter and oil in cooking. It is important to include some fat in your diet because fat gives you energy. It also helps your body to absorb some of the vitamins it needs.

JUST A LITTLE ...

You need to eat only a small amount of fat. If you eat too much, when your body has taken all the energy it needs, the rest of the fat is stored as 'body fat'. A little body fat is healthy, but too much fat can be unhealthy.

FOOD FACT

Everyone needs some body fat. Body fat keeps you warm, and is a good food store for emergencies. If you are sick and cannot eat, your body breaks down some of your body fat to give you energy until you can eat again.

GOOD FAT, BAD FAT

There are three main kinds of fat:
- **unsaturated fats**
- **saturated fats**
- **trans fats**

Unsaturated fats are found in oily fish, avocados, nuts and seeds. Certain types of oil, such as olive oil and sunflower oil, also contain unsaturated fats. Unsaturated fats reduce the amount of cholesterol in your blood and protect you from heart disease, so they are a healthier choice than saturated and trans fats.

Saturated fats usually come from animal sources, such as dairy foods or meat. Saturated fats and trans fats are also found in processed foods, such as pastries, cakes and biscuits. These types of fat are unhealthy because they can *increase* the amount of cholesterol in your blood. Over time, this can block your blood vessels and lead to heart disease.

OMEGA OILS

It is important to eat some foods that contain omega oils because they help do important things, such as keep your blood vessels healthy. Nuts and oily fish are good choices. Omega oils in fish have an added benefit – many scientists believe that they make your brain work better!

VITAMINS AND MINERALS

Vitamins and minerals are very important nutrients for good health. The great news is that, apart from sugar, most foods contain some vitamins or minerals. Eating a wide range of food will give you all you need.

VITAMINS

Every part of your body uses vitamins, which are known by letters of the alphabet. For example, vitamin A keeps your skin, hair and nails healthy. There are several kinds of vitamin B, such as B6 and B12. They all help you get energy from food. Vitamin C helps wounds to heal, and vitamin K helps your blood clot. Vitamin E helps you fight illness and disease.

MINERALS

Two of the most important minerals are calcium and iron. Calcium makes your bones and teeth strong and it helps your muscles to work. Milk and dairy products contain lots of calcium and other important minerals. Meat and sardines are rich in iron, which helps your blood take in oxygen. If you are low in iron, you may feel tired and ill.

SALT

Salt contains sodium, which is another kind of mineral. Your body needs some salt to work properly. Salt occurs naturally in many foods. However, many people eat much more salt than their body needs.

Some people add salt to food when they are cooking or to their finished meal. Ready-made meals usually contain a lot of salt to make them taste better. Crisps, processed meats and salted nuts are high in salt, too. If you like eating lots of these types of food, you are probably eating too much salt. You should eat no more than one teaspoon of salt altogether each day.

HEALTHY HINT

True flavour

Salt hides the true taste of food. If you stop adding salt to your food, you will soon be able to enjoy its real taste. If you want extra flavour, try adding lemon juice or herbs and spices instead.

REGULAR FIBRE

Fibre is the parts of fruit, vegetables and grains that your body cannot digest. It includes the husk of grains of wheat and the stringy bits in fruit and vegetables. Fibre is not a nutrient, but you need it to be healthy.

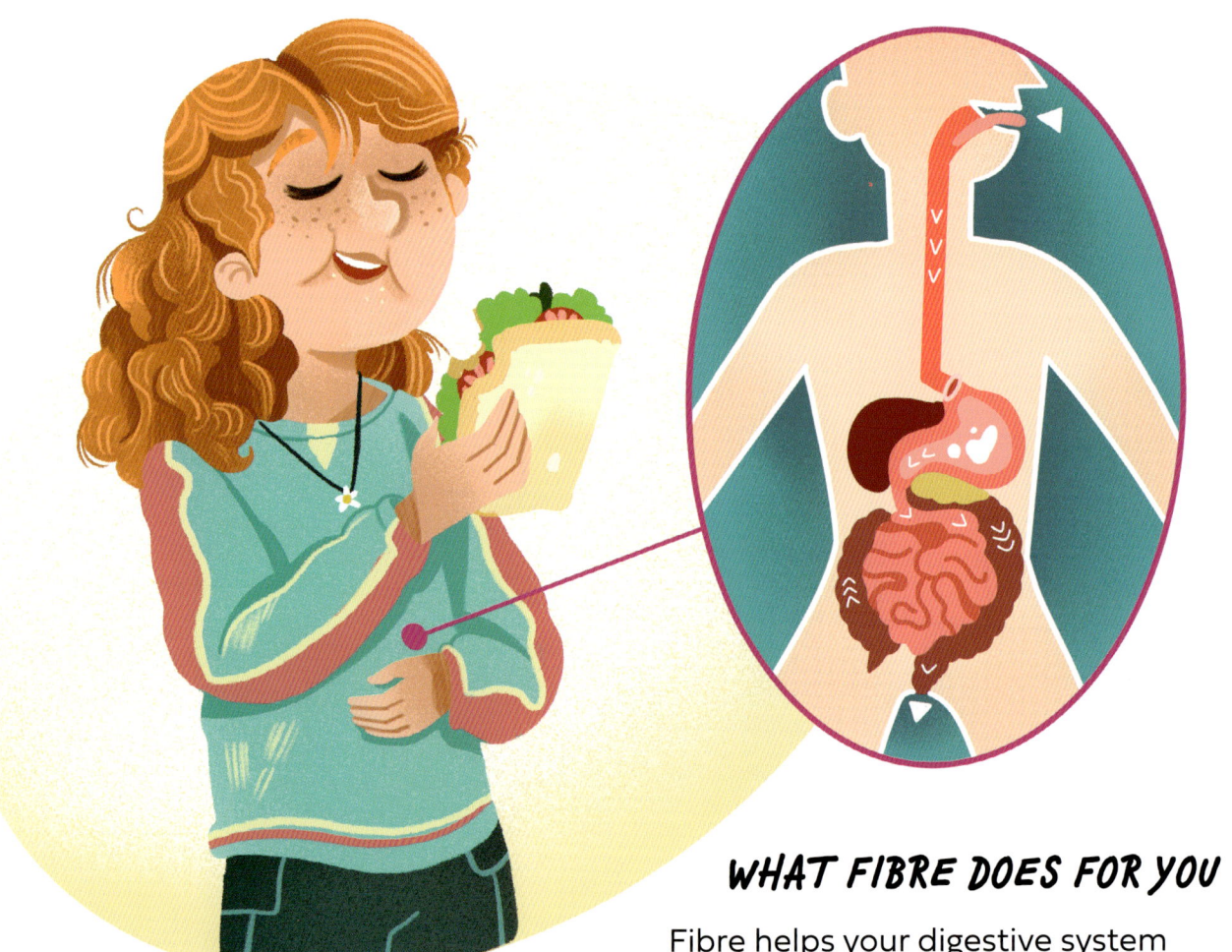

WHAT FIBRE DOES FOR YOU

Fibre helps your digestive system to work well. It is tough, so you need to chew it for longer. Chewing makes the rest of your food easier to digest. Fibre cannot be digested, so it makes your faeces (poo) softer and bulkier. That makes it easier to push faeces out of your body. If your diet is low in fibre, food will take longer to pass through your body. Your faeces may become dry, making them difficult to get rid of. This is called constipation.

FOODS RICH IN FIBRE

Vegetables are one of the best sources of fibre. Carrots, cabbage, broccoli and celery all contain lots of it. So do beans, lentils, peas and dried fruit, such as currants, figs and dates. Wholemeal bread and wholegrain food, such as brown rice and wholemeal pasta, are made with the whole of the grain, including the husk. They are high in fibre and are much healthier than white bread, white rice and food made with white flour.

FOOD FACT

Some people who eat beetroot can tell how long their food is taking to pass through their body, because the beetroot turns their faeces pink or red! Food usually takes between 12 and 36 hours to pass right through your digestive system.

WATER

Drinking water is very important because it helps to keep your body healthy. Two-thirds of your body is made up of water. Body fluids, such as blood and digestive juices, are mainly water. Your brain, muscles and other parts of your body contain water, too.

WATER LOSS

You lose water all the time, as sweat and urine (wee), in faeces and when you breathe out. To replace the water you lose, you should drink five or six glasses (1–1.5 litres) of water or other liquids a day.

HEALTHY HINT

Other drinks

When you're thirsty, the very best thing to drink is water. You could have sparkling water, or try adding lemon juice for flavour. Try to avoid sugary drinks, and limit fruit juice to one glass a day.

FOOD FACT

Watermelon is one of the most hydrating foods you can eat. Around 92 per cent of a watermelon is water!

WATER BALANCE

Your kidneys control the amount of water in your body. They clean your blood, removing some of the water and any substances your body does not need to make urine. The urine is stored in your bladder, until you empty it when you urinate. You can tell if you are drinking enough liquid because you should need to urinate once every two or three hours. If you do not urinate this often, or your urine is dark in colour, you need to drink more.

FEELING THIRSTY

If you do not drink enough liquid, you become dehydrated. When you are dehydrated, you may suffer from headaches, lack of concentration, tiredness and dizziness. You may find it hard to sleep properly. Normally, when your body is short of water, you feel thirsty and so you drink something. However, you can be dehydrated without feeling thirsty. This is why it is important to drink regularly throughout the day, whether you feel thirsty or not.

EATING TOO MUCH

To be as healthy as possible, it helps to be at the right body weight for your height. To maintain a healthy weight, you need to eat the right amount of food. It helps to do exercise, too. If you regularly eat more food that you need to, your body will store body fat. You will gradually become overweight.

OBESITY

Some people are obese. This means that they are very overweight. People who are obese can have some very serious health problems, such as heart disease, Type 2 diabetes and cancer. Obesity affects some people's mental health as well as their physical health.

HEALTHY HINT

Keep fit

Exercise helps people to stay at the right weight. To be fit and healthy, an average 11-year-old needs one hour's exercise a day. Walking, cycling, running and swimming are great choices.

LOSING WEIGHT

If you are overweight, it may take a bit of effort to get to a healthy weight. People who lose weight often feel fitter and healthier. A doctor or nutritionist can help people to lose weight by giving them information about what to do.

Making healthy food choices is the first step to being a healthy weight. Cutting out, or cutting down on, sweet and fatty foods is a great idea. Instead of eating sweets, you can eat fruit. Instead of using butter, you can use low-fat spreads. Instead of snacking on crisps, try snacking on vegetables. Eating food that is rich in fibre (see pages 18–19) helps you to feel full more quickly, too.

DIETING DANGERS

Some people go on special diets to lose weight quickly. This can be very unhealthy. Some diets do not provide all the nutrients you need. When you lose weight too quickly, you often gain the weight back, when you finish the diet. This is called 'yo-yo' dieting. By eating healthily most of the time you can avoid this type of dieting and maintain a healthy weight.

EATING TOO LITTLE

Eating too little can bring as many problems as eating too much. If people do not eat enough, they cannot get all the nutrients they need. Seriously underweight people can become very ill.

SIGNS AND SYMPTOMS

When people do not eat enough, they lose weight and become thin. People who are underweight may begin to have acne, too. Their hair becomes thinner and some of it may fall out. They may feel very tired and they do not have the energy they need to do everyday things, such as going to school or going out with friends.

HEALTHY HINT

Think positive

Sometimes, people see faults in themselves that no one else can see. Be kind to yourself and remember that no one is 'perfect'. Try to think positively about all the amazing things that your healthy body can do.

EATING DISORDERS

Sometimes, people have an eating disorder, such as anorexia or bulimia. Eating disorders can affect both boys and girls. Many people with eating disorders take extreme action to lose weight and may be very secretive or controlling around food. People who have eating disorders urgently need help from a doctor to help them tackle these mental health conditions.

ANOREXIA AND BULIMIA

People who suffer from anorexia do not eat enough. Because they don't eat enough they lose weight. If you lose too much weight, your organs, such as your heart, can't function properly, which can be very serious.

People who suffer from bulimia often eat plenty of food. However, they make themselves vomit soon after they have eaten. Vomiting regularly can cause stomach issues and tooth decay.

BODY FACT

Bodies come in all shapes and sizes. It is more important to be healthy than thin.

A HEALTHY DIET

A balanced diet is a healthy diet, where a variety of foods are eaten every day.

HOW MUCH FOOD DO PEOPLE NEED?

Boys and men, on average, are taller and heavier than girls and women of the same age. Because of this, they may need to eat more to make sure that they get all the energy they need.

Children and young people need lots of nutrients, because they are growing. Therefore, they need to eat more than adults, who have reached their final height.

People who exercise a lot also need to eat more than others, because exercise burns energy more quickly than other activities. Often, as people become older, they are less active and their metabolism slows down. This is why older people often eat less than young people.

CHOOSING HEALTHY FOODS

Food is healthiest when it is natural (unprocessed). Fresh fruit is healthier than a fruit snack bar. Chicken breast is healthier than chicken nuggets. Processed foods often have added ingredients and some of them may not be good for you.

For example, beans are a healthy source of protein. Baked beans from a can are not quite as healthy, because they may have added sugar or salt. It is easy to eat too much salt, sugar and fat when you eat lots of processed food.

HEALTHY OR UNHEALTHY?

Which of these foods are healthier choices? Which are unhealthy?
- **wholemeal bread**
- **hot dogs**
- **fizzy drinks**
- **sugary cereals**
- **fresh fruit salad**
- **vegetables**
- **rice**
- **milk**
- **chips.**

Answers on page 31

HEALTHY HINT

Check the label

You can read food labels on processed food packaging to see exactly what is in the food. Food labels tell you at a glance how much carbohydrate, protein, fat, sugar and salt food contains. They can help you to make the healthiest choices.

MAKE A HEALTHY PIZZA!

Pizzas are delicious, but having takeaway fast foods is not usually the healthiest choice to make. Here is a quick, easy way to make your own healthy pizza. This pizza uses wholemeal pitta bread for the base, for extra fibre. Add your own favourite extras to the healthy cheese and tomato topping.

Warning: All cooking is to be done with adult supervision and help. Check all ingredients in advance. If you are allergic to any ingredients suggested, do not use them.

INGREDIENTS
(TO MAKE FOUR PIZZAS)

For the base:
4 wholemeal pitta breads

For the topping:
1 can of chopped tomatoes
100g grated cheese (choose reduced-fat Cheddar or Parmesan cheese, if you can)

Topping extras:
Choose your favourites from these healthy foods:

Protein-rich extras:
Tuna, cooked prawns or cooked chicken, pine nuts, mozzarella cheese.

Vegetarian extras: Sliced red or green peppers, pineapple, olives, sweetcorn, mushrooms, spinach, sliced onion, basil.

TO MAKE YOUR PIZZAS ...

1. Heat the oven to 200°C/400°F/Gas mark 6.
2. Cover the pitta breads with a layer of chopped tomatoes, followed by a layer of grated cheese.
3. Now add your favourite topping extras. Include at least one choice from protein-rich extras and one choice from vegetarian extras.
4. Sprinkle a second, lighter layer of grated cheese over the top.
5. Put the pizza in the oven. Cook for 20 minutes. Remove and enjoy when it is cool enough to eat!

QUIZ

How healthy is the food you eat? Try this quick quiz to find out.

1. You have overslept and you are running late for school. Do you:
a) Skip breakfast?
b) Grab a doughnut on your way to school?
c) Drink a glass of milk and take a banana or a slice of bread to eat on the way?

2. You are really thirsty. Which of these drinks are you most likely to choose:
a) A carton of juice?
b) A can of fizzy drink?
c) A bottle of water?

3. You are eating out. Which option is the healthiest for you to choose:
a) Spaghetti bolognese, followed by ice cream?
b) Burger and chips, followed by chocolate cake?
c) Fish with vegetables, followed by fruit?

4. You are hungry when you get home from school. Do you:
a) Have some more breakfast cereal?
b) Grab a packet of crisps and a chocolate biscuit?
c) Chop up some fruit and vegetables to dip into yoghurt or hummus?

5. You decide to make a meal for your family. Do you:
a) Heat up some frozen pizzas and serve them with salad?
b) Heat up a ready-made meal from the supermarket?
c) Cook some chicken or lentils with vegetables and serve with rice?

Answers on page 31

Glossary

acne A skin problem that causes spots on the face or body

anorexia An eating disorder in which people restrict what they eat to the point where they can become dangerously thin and ill

bacteria Tiny single-celled organisms that can only be seen through a microscope. Some bacteria cause disease

bulimia An eating disorder in which people vomit or use laxatives after eating to the point where they can become dangerously thin and ill

calcium A mineral found in some foods, especially milk

cholesterol A fatty substance found in your blood. Too much can be dangerous for the health of your heart

chyme A fluid mixture of stomach acid and partly-digested food

dehydrated Having lost a lot of water from the body

eating disorder A mental health condition, such as anorexia or bulimia

faeces Poo

fibre The substance found in some foods which travels through the digestive system quickly and easily

food groups Groups of foods that contain similar nutrients; there are five main food groups

husk The outer covering of cereal grains

hydrating something that provides a lot of water

iron A mineral found in some foods, such as beef and spinach

large intestine The part of the digestive system that produces faeces. The large intestine connect to the small intestine at one end and the anus at the other

laxatives Substances that help to get faeces out of someone's body

minerals Substances, such as calcium and iron, that your body needs to be healthy

nutrients Parts of food that your body uses to get energy and to work properly

nutritionist A person who advises what people should eat to be healthy

omega oil The oil found in some fish, such as salmon and tuna, and in nuts and seeds, which is essential to good health

processed food Food that has been changed from its natural state, such as chicken nuggets or baked beans

proteins Nutrients that the body uses to build organs. It is found in foods such as meat and fish

saliva Watery liquid produced in the mouth that helps to break down food and start the digestion process

saturated fats Animal fat, such as butter or the fat on meat

small intestine The part of the digestive system where food is digested and absorbed into the blood. The small intestine connects to the stomach at one end and the large intestine at the other

trans fats Very unhealthy fats that are made when liquid oils are turned into solid fats and then used to make food products, such as cakes and pies

unsaturated fats Oil or fat that comes from plants, such as avocados, nuts and olives.
urine Wee

Quiz answers

Mostly a:
You often choose the easy option, which may be unhealthy. Try to practise healthier habits.

Mostly b:
You really need to think about healthy eating. At the moment, you are choosing unhealthy foods. Try reading this book again to get some more ideas.

Mostly c:
Well done! You are choosing healthy foods that will help you feel good! If you want to find out more, try looking at the books and websites on page 31.

Answers from page 27

HEALTHY OR UNHEALTHY?

Wholemeal bread, fresh fruit salad, vegetables, rice and milk are healthy choices. Hot dogs, fizzy drinks, sugary cereals and chips are unhealthy choices.

Index

acne 24

bacteria 11
blood 4, 5, 8, 9, 10, 16, 20, 21
body fat 14, 15, 22
body weight 22
bones 5, 16
brain 20
bread 5, 6, 8, 19

caffeine 21
calcium 16
carbohydrates 5, 6, 8, 25, 27
cereals 6
cholesterol 15
constipation 18

dairy 6, 7, 16
digestive system 18
drinks 21

eating disorders 25
eggs 7, 13
energy 8–9, 10, 15, 16, 24, 26
exercise 8, 22, 23, 25, 26

faeces 5, 18, 19, 20
fat 6, 7, 14–15, 25, 27
fibre 6, 10, 18–19, 23
fish 5, 6, 13, 15, 16
food groups 6
fruit 6, 7, 18, 23, 25, 27

glucose 8, 9
gum disease 11

hair 5, 12, 16, 24

illness 15, 16
iron 16

meat 6, 12, 14, 16
minerals 6, 7, 16–17
muscles 12, 16, 20

nails 16
nutrients 4, 5, 6, 8, 10, 13, 16, 23, 24, 26

obesity 22
oils 7, 14, 15
omega oils 13, 15

protein 5, 6, 7, 12–13, 25, 27

salt 13, 17, 27
skin 12, 16
slimming diets 23
snacks 9
starch 8, 9
sugar 6, 7, 9, 10–11, 16, 25, 27

teeth 11, 16

urine 20, 21

vegan 6, 7, 13
vegetables 6, 18, 19, 23
vegetarians 6, 7, 13
vitamins 6, 7, 14, 16

water 20–21